A city called normality

Kunal Kondhare

BookLeaf Publishing

A city called normality © 2023 Kunal Kondhare

All rights reserved.

No part of this publication may be reproduced, stored in a retrieval system, or transmitted, in any form or by any means, electronic, mechanical, photocopying, recording or otherwise, without the prior written permission of the presenters.

Kunal Kondhare asserts the moral right to be identified as author of this work.

Presentation by *BookLeaf Publishing*

Web: www.bookleafpub.com

E-mail: info@bookleafpub.com

ISBN: 9789357740272

First edition 2023

To my creator, aai.

ACKNOWLEDGEMENT

I would like to thank first and foremost my friend Siddharth who introduced me to this opportunity, which made this book possible. Then I would like to thank my mentor Dr. Jyuthika Laghate whose relentless efforts have allowed me to use whatever poetic skills I possessed. I would also like to thank the Bookleafpublishing team for such a great opportunity.

Finally, I'd like to thank my late mother, without whom my existence was impossible, and without her inspiration, nothing would've been possible.

PREFACE

This book is a collection of my attempt at English poetry. This book describes human emotions in various ways, may it be being out at sea, or feeling grief, or cherishing old memories or finding your tinder. This will be a perfect read for readers of any age.

Broken

Lost some friends
Went with the trend

Straightened every curve on the bend
For you, I made so many ammends

Yet you broke my heart and left me crying
People told me this is life,
But I'm screaming,
I'm dying.

Alone

Four walls, a table, and one chair.
These were my companions, as I took my mind
for a wander
I knew I had time to squander.

Through the lush green meadows in a far off
land
And feel the salty breeze on my face, and the
warm beach sand.

I met many a people, and travelled through
many a land, some were outlandishly poor, and
somewhere unusually grand.

Yet I never found the comfort, I was looking for
it was the comfort I had run from.

A comfort in which I was never left alone, a
comfort called home.

Friendship

We're kids when we make the promises of
forever
It isn't until we're older that we know its bound
to end.

No matter what you do
How hard you try
It will come to an end

Perhaps you'll go on different paths
The long conversations will be cut short

Your times together will see a downtrend
Until they're nothing but a legend

You'll then know it's come to an end
And that it's time to find a new Friend

Community

You, I, him and they
We make a community

We have no boundary, we're in every
Gully, village and city

Today hatred is beyond control
Why not make it our only goal?

Why not make a difference in people's lives
Create a place where happiness thrives?

A place where money doesn't matter more than
lives

A place where humanity survives

Certain

I was walking down a lonesome road with quite
certainty

A road which wasn't easy neither was pretty

Yet I had been hard ,gritty and full of alacrity
For I had with me the opinions of the witty

All I wanted was to prosper that too in
anonymity

But mites crept in with acquity , giving my
decisions a sense of animosity
Disturbing all the equanimity

Just to let me know
Life is a game of just another possibility
With just one constituent, called uncertainty .

Nothing matters

We are young, filled with confidence to the
brim!!
Making bold moves with days passing
Thriving to keep the close ones laughing
Planning, fighting, one day the world we shall
conquer and earn everything!!
Facing obstacles and yet striving
We will be driving ourselves to the
Peak as we go down the cliff to the very end

We feel we've earned something
There's no need to keep working.
But the fact is we've gained nothing.
And lost EVERYTHING.

Then & Now

Then, we were boys with lots of friends and
huge ambitions
Now we are men with no friends and huge egos

Then we wanted to grow up
Now we want to be a child

Then we had happy evenings, now we have
sleepless nights!!

Then we were happy from the bottom of our
hearts
Now we are broken and lonely to the very heart

Then we had a childhood
Now we have a past!!

Then we believed in love
And yet after all these years we still believe in
love!!

Cause times change
People remain the same
Cause just moments are lost
Memories are not!!

A city called Normality

I was walking down a lonesome road with quite
certainty…
A road called life which wasn't easy nor pretty.
And I went to a city called normality.

Here being heavier is called obesity
You must belong to a religious fraternity
You're also judged by your sensuality
And homosexuality is met with atrocity

You get looked down upon just for frugality
Cause here being rich is the only normality

To survive here you must have a certain quality
called hypocriticality
Such as "virtually fight" for equality
Yet in reality point out every single dissimilarity

Here social media is the hyper reality
If you prefer not to use it, you're just an
"abnormality"
Your follower list is preferred over brotherhoods
and "unity"

Here your amity must only be a morality

For you must be love capitalist inhumanity
To fit into this "normality"
Or be cast out just as another abnormality

Here you must embrace irrationality
In your every meal you must have theatricality
Or suffer being the abnormality

Being different here is just "insanity"
For the most important aspect of living here is
commonality
Here no one accepts the actuality
They "refuse" diversity
Proceed to look for "cures" and "superiority"

All this city gives you is duality,
Their hospitality is just a formality,
Waiting for you to turn your back so that they
can unleash their normality
Or better put "brutality".

This city called normality has a very
narrow-minded mentality
It has stolen all my alacrity with animosity…
For now all I wish is mortality
Or
Go to a city far far away where diversity is not
an abnormality
Perhaps a city called synchronicity.

Virtuality

Today, As we lose ourselves in the realms of
virtual reality, or virtuality should I say

That we forget the realms of actual reality, and
perhaps humanity!

We forget the days we met for actual cricket,
and didn't take any "ingame" Wickets

The days when we stole mangoes and jumped
pickets, instead of stealing kills from unrealistic
snippets.

Then friends used to meet every fortnight,
today they meet on 'Fortnite'

Then pub was a place for having fun, now
nothing's changed except for a extra g and that's
the pun.

Thus about the gen next I worry, will the ever
live really or die a mere virtuality.

Our Story

I didn't know if I wanted it.
I did doubt it for a little bit

But you made all the doubts go away.
I'm a bird, I tell you, eager to fly away. I jump
from branch to branch, thinking of my life
ahead, but somehow without thinking of you, I
can't go to bed.

You're like a daydream, that refuses to leave.
You're the agrarian that provides me with the
prettiest view

Beyond the superficiality, you're an inspiration.
For me you're my daily dose of motivation

I know you aren't perfect, and you've got your
flaws. But that's what makes you interesting,
and anyways perfect isn't in natures laws!

Your furtive eyes tell me a thousand tales, I get
lost in them without fail, your guileless voice
has a sacrosant hold, which makes me warm and
fuzzy in the heart when I'm cold.

This isn't a ballad of your praises, but a story
made from a thousand gazes. Since the years,
I've known you, I've counted them all,
sometimes wondering, if it meant anything at all.

I kept on thinking, I'd wait for the right time, but
the time would be right, when, I'm yours and
you're mine.

Desire

Today, desire consumed me again
The desire to control, the desire to feel whole

It made me do inexplicable things
It made me drink
It made me push you to the brink of your being

It made me deaf to your cries and screams

But, but I love you, and it wasn't me
Today, desire consumed me

Grief

15

Grief is a companion we must all have
Grief is an enemy we must all face.

Grief doesn't check if you're a hero with a cape
or a mere college kid with a vape!

Grief doesn't have any form face or shape.
But it comes from a loss though, a parent, a
relationship or a broken pencil case.

No matter who we are, we must go through it
and we MUST grow through it.

Grief makes you lonely standing in a crowd.
Grief makes you silent, when you want to
scream out loud.

Grief is like a creeper growing on your tree.
If you don't uproot it, it will scavenge on you for
free.

But if you're strong enough, grief cannot forever
cloud your mind, and if you look at the little
things in life, you will see sunshine.

This is Hell

No one can threaten me about it cause
This is hell

In the heinous crimes, grim times I know
This is hell

In the white lies and pain filled cries I know
This is hell

In the turmoil and fruitless toil I know
This is hell

Keep your temples and your heaven to yourself

You can't scare me, I know
This is hell

Men

Men don't cry
Men don't feel
Men should possess hearts of steel

Any emotion must be locked away
All signs of "weakness" shook away

Men can't be weak
Men can't let a tear leak

Men should be emotionless
Men should be strong
Anything else is straight out wrong

Is this the price of masculinity?
To shoulder every responsibility?

The world talks so much about equality
When will it look at this toxicity?

No Cry

Drink up your tears, and do not cry

There's a future staring at you, you must achieve
it, or atleast try!!

There is a past that haunts you everyday
Tis a nightmare that won't let you stay!

But no, do not weep and cry
Go fight your battle
Wear your past like your armour

A rising sun awaits you, its goldenrays shining
upon the brightest gems of your future.

Child

19

Don't do that!
Don't run wild!

Oh! You can't be that loud, be soft and mild!

Don't run on the grass!! Stop trying to slide!

Now it's acceptable to lie and be lied
It's appalling how difficult it is to be a child!

Where are you?

Is there a God? If so where is he, or is it a she?

Are you up in the sky, hiding behind those
flowing clouds?
Or are you higher above in the throngs of blue?

Do you flow with the air like many believe?
Or do you glow in the sunny glare, leaving a
crimson hue?

Are you in the children, running around with
innocent glee?
Or are you hiding up the banyan tree?

Are you in the strong big boulders we see,
Or are you in the dust that flows free?

Are you really an entity?
Or just a concept, created to make money?

The sea

Have you ever been to the sea?
It's like a world of fantasy

The calming, yet dangerous waves
Tell the stories of far off lands, they
Rise and fall
As if his hands

The saltiness in the breeze, gives you a freshness
like a cup of tea as you stare into the depths of
the sea.

The ships sail faraway beyond the horizon
Leaving pretty sights, for us to ponder on

The sea teaches us a lesson
The lesson of being calm and free

Enclosed under this calmness however
Lies a monster waiting to be unleashed
Destroying everything it can see

Have you ever been to the sea?

Rebel

He'll want a no when it's a yes
When asked to be neat, he'll create a mess

He'll do things that'll land him in jail
But he'll he himself even in that prison cell

He'll run across the road
And skid on the grass

He'll know societal norms are trash
He'll always be high on life, not caring for the
crash

You can yearn for heaven, he'll happily choose
hell

That's what you call a classic rebel

Depression

On dark lonely nights, it jumps on you
On bright sunny days it creeps on you

It's called depression, it feeds on you
Depression is the loneliness amongst friends
It's the overthinking to no ends…

Depression is the days you spent crying
It's the mares in which you were flying

Straight into boulders, wanting a hard shoulder
Yet somehow, still wanting to go headfirst

It's like wanting to be saved and to be hurt

It'll consume you, making you it's slave
Twisting your reality, until you run to your
mind's darkest cave.

It's a dark creature; wanting to make you its
own.
Eyeing up the opportunity to find in you its new
home.

Life goes on

Life isn't as dramatic as it's made out to be

We're brought up with the idea of wild and free

But life is just simple, it goes on

Someone might hit rockbottom, but life doesn't
care, it goes on

Someone might be a philanthropist, but life goes
on

Someone might discover protons and neutrons,
but life doesn't care, it goes on

Someone dies and life is supposed to get
distorted and broken, but life doesn't care, it
goes on.

In a moment, something great is done, and life is
expected to change forever, but the moment
passes and life goes on

Life is supposed to be an adventure of sorts
But life's just simple, it goes on.

www.ingramcontent.com/pod-product-compliance
Lightning Source LLC
LaVergne TN
LVHW021338200726
843509LV00014B/2572